MW00743939

THE *Fabric*
OF *Day*

NEW AND SELECTED POEMS

ALSO BY ANNE CAMPBELL

POETRY

No Memory of a Move, Longspoon 1983, Newest 1985
Death is an Anxious Mother, Thistledown, 1986
Red Earth, Yellow Stone, Thistledown, 1989
Angel Wings All Over, Thistledown, 1994
Soul to Touch, Hagios, 2009

NON-FICTION, CO-EDITED

Regina's Secret Spaces, Love and Lore of Local Geography, 2006
Biblio Files, A History of the Regina Public Library, 2017

THE *Fabric* OF *Day*

NEW AND SELECTED POEMS

ANNE CAMPBELL

thistledown press

©Anne Campbell, 2017
All rights reserved

No part of this publication may be reproduced or transmitted in any form or by any means, graphic, electronic or mechanical, including photocopying, recording, or any information storage and retrieval system, without permission in writing from the publisher or a licence from The Canadian Copyright Licensing Agency (Access Copyright). For an Access Copyright licence, visit www.accesscopyright.ca or call toll free to 1-800-893-5777.

Thistledown Press Ltd.
410 2nd Avenue North
Saskatoon, Saskatchewan, S7K 2C3
www.thistledownpress.com

Library and Archives Canada Cataloguing in Publication

Campbell, Anne, 1938-
[Poems. Selections]
The fabric of day : new and selected poems / Anne Campbell.

ISBN 978-1-77187-130-3 (softcover)
I. Title. II. Title: Poems. Selections.

PS8555.A5272A6 2017   C811'.54   C2017-901109-X

Cover photograph: *Grasslands National Park, East Block* by Don Hall
Cover and book design by Jackie Forrie
Printed and bound in Canada

Canada Council   Conseil des Arts
for the Arts   du Canada

SASKATCHEWAN
ARTS BOARD

Canada

Thistledown Press gratefully acknowledges the financial assistance of the Canada Council for the Arts, the Saskatchewan Arts Board, and the Government of Canada for its publishing program.

ACKNOWLEDGEMENTS

So many to acknowledge, and thank: my thoughtful editor, Doug Barbour; photographer Don Hall, for his exquisite expression of the prairie, and long-time friendship; early readers of my work over the years, Doug (DG) Jones, and my sister, Leona King. Special thanks to Thistledown Press for this book, *The Fabric of Day*, and for their years of support with earlier books, *Death is an Anxious Mother*; *Red Earth, Yellow Stone*; and, *Angel Wings All Over*. Thanks to Hagios Press for permission to reprint poems from *Soul to Touch*, and to Longspoon and NeWest Press for for my first book, *No Memory of a Move*.

Thank you to my family all: Jill and Ken; Jacqueline and Bob; Joe and Ronda; and the next generation to whom this book is dedicated. Thanks to my King siblings and their families: Ken and Marilyn; Rick and Barb; Ron and Katherine; Raymond, and Leona. Thanks to Don and Andrea, Audrey, Jeannie, Luella, Nijole, Allister, Cyril and Helene, Kathleen, and Nicolle, for the constancy of their friendship. Thanks too for my Croatian cousins, and for those many other friends and colleagues who have enriched my life. And lastly, this book is in memory of my friend, Jacquie Stewart.

Thank you too for the following publications where earlier versions of poems appeared:

Anthologies: *Writing Right, Poetry by Canadian Women*, Longspoon, 1982; *Glass Canyons*, On Calgary, fiction and poetry, NeWest, 1985; *Dancing Visions*, Thistledown, 1985; *A Sudden Radiance*, Coteau, 1987; *Out of Place*, Coteau, 1991; *What is Already Known*, Thistledown, 1995; *In the Clear*, Thistledown, 1998; *Listening with the Ear of the Heart*, St. Peter's Press, 2003

Journals, including: *NeWest*, *Quarry*, *Northward Journal*, *Descant*, *Dandelion*, *Grain*, *Island*, *Canadian Forum*, *Labrys-Bran's Head* at Hunting Raven Press, England, *Poetry Canada Review*, *Prairie Fire*, *Event*, *The Globe & Mail*.

For Jocelyn; Sarah; Thomas, little River and Shayla; Brent; and Alden and Trenna

Contents

DEATH IS AN ANXIOUS MOTHER, 1986

RED EARTH, YELLOW STONE, 1989

ANGEL WINGS ALL OVER, 1994

SOUL TO TOUCH, 2009

THE FABRIC OF DAY, *NewPoems*

On Time, an introduction

Someone asked, "Looking back, what were you writing about?"

And I looked back: book by book; poem by poem; did a word search, saw images repeating, and it was my prairie land that emerged — beginning in *No Memory of a Move*, 1983, where "grass and me (were) equal," moved through the other books, firmed up in *Soul to Touch*, 2009, and continued into the new poems in this book.

And if the image most often appearing is prairie, the word most often recurring is "time," the air we breathe, the space within which we live. For me, the prairie is not empty, but filled with the salient, uninterrupted, air we breathe, pulling us into the fullness of each moment, one after another.

And indoors the poems become exchange with every day; with birds, and music and dreams; with a family wedding, family funerals, a friend's art work, even shelf paper; our own Leonard Cohen gets a mention, as does the archaeologist, Wade Davis, who mourns the loss of voice from lands where languages have gone missing; Heidegger appears, sharing a view with prairie farmers. In one poem, from *Death is an Anxious Mother*, a monk says, " . . . for constipation, eat popcorn; for God, look everywhere." Everything is inhabited with time.

There is pain; but like the prairie there is endurance; and if not joy, there seems to remain, always, the questions; to which awe, at the mystery in which we find ourselves, is the answer.

No Memory of a Move

Longspoon Press, 1983; Newest Press1985

PINE POEMS

1.

All right
this is the beginning
no more
pissin in the wind
  (I might have   got it
      wrong, the sex there)   but

the point is : it's time
      to begin   back
      before
  pine scent   back before

     the memory of pine
        quickens
          in me

    pictures: parents holding hands
      haloed in trees
         looking up   together
               in the camera
and the other one   my mother
  posing   paddling alone in a canoe
      on their honeymoon   or

      is it   me
I remember in Saskatoon the pine scent
       just begins there

2.

The car is old
always square
so long after
others were rounded
and it's always   black
I remember one — Willys Knight

we are on our way
north
packed   in it
for the trip
from Saskatoon

the road
when we arrive
near the farm   is corduroy covered
logs rolled over muskeg   am I always
the only one   awake   the oldest one
awakened   when we rattle over it
just before the turn   aunt
uncles are there   but
I remember   gold
my grandmother   kerosene lamps
an oval   soft round place   and
     being held there
   sleeping in a loft   my mother
     settling us down   myself
       barely able   to lie
still   containing tomorrow

     pine scent
         stirring me
through the night

3.

The well
was a story
picture in a book

logs made the base
an arc held the crank

milk was in the pail
my grandfather
slowly wound down
hot July
afternoons

he said:
don't touch the rope
never touch the pail
the worst thing is the risk
contaminating

the well

draws me

knowledge
to the fall

nine year old   arms
skinny
can't control   the crank

milk whitens
water in the well

4.

We tried to be
like   country kids
watching movies   in town
old Tom Mix   serials
Saturday afternoon

sisters
on holiday   from the city
watching   mixed up
blurry film
confused   we stay

through the afternoon
the film goes on and on

5.

The puzzle
even then
over peace: wanting to stir

sitting
in the sun
alone
on a fence   crossed over
wide   english style
no wind
thinking   I should think
this is perfect
aware

I am waiting
even then
for a care

8. Memory of a move

St. Joseph's School
in Saskatoon   (when I was 4 or 5)
is now
a school of   Native Survival

out for a ride
old black car   then   only
partly filled (3 of 7   kids still to come)
it was   touchstone
warm red   brick
a place   she always said
where you will go   then

there is an absence
we are somewhere   else and I am in
another school

what is this
constant memory   what metaphor is here

over it again   and again
the bare elements
are:
a child   in black
car   passing
school   mother saying
the words   an interruption

memory of an absence
no memory of a move

OLD COUNTRY PAINTING

My grandmother's sister dressed all in black
with babushka and old country ways
midmorning each day when she finishes her   chores
puts her husband carefully outside

Settling him there on a chair with his cane
beside a red house warmed by the sun
she moves to her place
just to his left and slightly aside

Some travellers passing by
note: deep into dusk   the couple
        who   remain there.

HOW THE DAY WAS BEGUN

The house was not as large
                    as at first
                         I thought   and
in the kitchen
                    my tiny grandmother
never going to bed or getting up
was always by the stove
                              mornings
my grandfather   Big Paul
would come down the stairs
                         slowly
          sit at the long kitchen table
          eating polenta
          his huge moustache
          rolling

He would listen to the news broadcast
               roll a Vogue cigarette

               then he would rise   strike a match
               and begin
               the day

THE ACROBATS OF CANTON VISIT HERITAGE PARK, CALGARY

            Two buses
                filled with Chinese
    arrive   (and I'm nervous about how best to please them)
            This Park
                    this historical park
                soft on warm days
                    today
                    is cold.

                    But we begin
                down the hill
                    always first   to the Wainwright, frontier hotel
            inside we look through glass doors to
                    mannequins
                        dressed as doctors, patients
                                travelling men and
                        wedding couples
                (this takes a total of 12 of 60 minutes)

    Out on the street
            still it is cold   but
    70 Chinese are laughing
        taking turns
                wearing white hats
            they are cowboys
                photographing each other
    in front of Gledhills drugstore

finding
each others spirit   we are
smiling but
refrain
from embracing
one another
Easy
now
I   decide to show off
our carriage collection
unlock the front door
the carriages
are upstairs   and down
there   on the spur
of the moment
I push open the big double back doors
outside
The Burnside Ranch,
wheat stooked
highland cattle grazing
Percheron horses dozing   sheep, ducks and pigs,
unfolds
storybook
before us   Wheat, I point, forgetting myself, proud.
Ducks, I hear   a woman's voice and in a wave
we go forth.
Canadian ducks bigger, the woman says.
We are pleased with each other.
Ranchman Helge chases up some pigs for watching
I show the Duck woman a sod house   say
This is   how some early settlers lived
she tells the others
who laugh.

Walking back
        she puts her hands
            close together
says   Canadian history   very short
            Very short   I say.

    North West Mounted Police Barracks, Weedon School
        we see through their windows
                trading now   school for "shi shou"
        We're having fun
        when the tour   organizer   says
                It's cold for Chinese
                    time to go.

        They'll give me a lift
            back to the gate

            Tony, Chinese
                in our office
                has prepared   me
                "chi chin"   see you again

I practise   under my breath   riding to the top
        and at the top
        I stand
        you could say
                in love
            my "chi chin"   ready
    see you again
                    caught
        in their sudden clapping
                goodbye

LOVE SONG ONE

with thanks to Hawthorne

You said   one day
Do you know the story
of the man
who had a perfect lover   except
for a mole on her cheek   and I said
no.

It is said   he was so troubled
by   his lover's flaw
he wanted to remove it.   He
searched and he dug   going deeper and deeper
but when finally he got to the root   and got it out
he found it was her heart   he had
instead
you said.

OK

I've come home
alone   tonight
and that's right   I'm
acting like a fool   I
have all anyone can ask   for
you make love like no one else   can
think what I have to say   the greatest
but tonight   your boyishness won't work   and
I am deeply attracted   to my chosen
idea of a man   who is just as deeply attracted
to an ideal   woman of his own   and
that leaves you and me   out   cold   but
we've been here one or two times   before   and
at least I know by now one or two things   not to do
       in fact you see
       I absent myself
           absinthe myself
assure myself   by morning   it will be gone   and
sure enough   by morning
       there is a message
         from my reptilian brain
            calling me   to curl up   in a corner
            lie inside where it is warm
        and with this message
         I am   back
           falling into my idea
          of a great big grown up
            man

OTHER MAN

I reach for you
    more tentative than I was
      with that first man
want to touch
              across a table in the Novia Cafe
but instead we sit
        talk
hear a man call a friend on a phone
    when he leaves
            we go on talking
while a Chinese waitress
                sweeping the floor
closes one section
        after another

THE ANSWER

Spirit
you see   in me
but
it's in you
I've detected
(Does this
make you
blush)
delicacy   spirit   (oh
I admit you   try to
shout it
down)
admit
with you
such sweetness
(that word
that sweetness   word)
I hope it
does it   not intrude   or   perhaps
with love   you will   permit   an image
: your
spirit
delicate
as light

brushing
the middle of me
song   so long asleep
open

QUEER CORNERED CAP

Absolutely not
no more
not today
I'm finished
that's it
no more acting like a fool.

Resolution lasts   forever
well til noon   or
when I see you
whichever happens first

Trouble is :   I admit this direction,
my inclination
towards the fool
is one to which I feel
quite naturally inclined

I have always had a secret yen
to wear
a queer cornered cap
flop about in velvet
lie around the floor
mouth witty schisms
kick up my heels
It's gone so far   I imagine
turning upside down
legs hooked over door
caps bells ringing wildly
me   swinging
back and forth
singing
high   in the wind

OLD LOVERS

The best thing
about old lovers   is now
when you meet them
on the street   you can
throw your arms around them
hug them   kiss them
hold them to pieces
no worries   now
they're
cousins   uncles
brothers

and sons.

THE MAGICIAN

I've got myself
a certain order
my life   somewhat straightened out
relationships
coming   one at a time
                              and
like Solomon   I think
he said it best
I am back
at Square Number
One
      Nothing really changed
                              oh maybe
head a little clear
                  less crowded in the heart
but life still a mystery
no love on Cloud Number Nine   yet   yet
                              there is a difference
                        someone has done a trick
mystery has become   my brother
enfolds me with care
I love   am different
my worry   has begun   to pale.

UNION

for E. J. Pratt

This idea
so large
of a place   and a time
before
we were lost from one another
sky   great seas   men and
women   still longing
   so strong
   we draw
   indifferent men
   to our breasts
   demand them
   alive
   carry them
   deep
   back
   home

HOME FEAR

My home is
        the north is / an idea
pine smell
        catching me / unaware
                    locking me
    into ice
        cold winter

THE DANCER

She sat on the flat brown ground
the only shape barely elevated
on land.
Looking to the left she could see in the distance
small and circular/gusts of dust
a miniature cyclone.
As the circle came closer/she saw it contained
a woman/moving upward as high in the air
as she moved forward in dance.
Without effort she was danced
over land through air in the rhythm
of the woman who watched.

EDGING OUT

I am edging out
of the way I think
I like to look
         my hair
creeping out of combs
            my blouse
inching out
      of my skirt
which is turning
          just ever so slightly
                   off centre
and I notice
      the heels of my shoes
are wearing down
         at what I see
is not so unusually odd
        an angle

THE THERAPIST

My friend
      told me about a woman
he said was a basket case
                        whose doctor said had colitis
whose priest said
           had sinned
whose social worker said had marriage problems
who
      only felt herself to be
                    in pain
      for Christ's sake

HEMICRANIA
for all the migraines

Inside
the right side
of my head
a heavy darkness
growing larger
is putting   pressure on me
to move out

Aching blackness
crowding forward
is

slipping
down
and rolling
back around
itself
a black hole
gathering   weight
heavier
than
time

MID NIGHT TRYST

The angel of D.
and I
grappled
late last night
(about 3:25 a.m.)

or now I think
that's who
it was

at the time
all was a whirr
feathers   flying
me falling
a feeling
of confusion

but before
(I woke up)
it was   not really   sweet
but something
somewhat like that
a feeling
    hard to define
     or order
or remember
being   real

THE GOD OF ENCOUNTER

It was not mystical, the experience
(I want you to know)

that followed her waking
late that night. The waking itself
    the same as before,
                reality shifted
          sweating, sick at . . .
but I go on too long, you understand.
Suffice it to say: it was the same.
Forty years and still
              no understanding
the why of the shaking, the way of it
but this time (perhaps the 67th)
in the instant of it
           this time
the giving up
        Admitting:
             I can't go on alone
Said, only that not
             (this time) with
But what will happen to me.
            Only
I can't go on alone.
      Then
the room   filling with it
   (circus clown on stilts calling down
remember me, remember me or ballet mistress
back of stage catching nervous dancer's eyes)
      the room full
     filling the woman   quietly known

THE IMAGE

She was ironing when it came to her that
the division she saw in the world and which plagued her
would not be resolved by looking out, it came to her that
the division she saw was within

                                and then she remembered
that morning, sitting at mass, seeing it
from a consciously detached point of view, a heart
torn nearly in two, stricken she thought long ago
the imposition perhaps remembered though not its cause.
Then she saw the parts being drawn close together
loosely sewn by hand, the stitches dissolving
into the heart as it healed.

JEES LORD DON'T SHE JUGGLE GOOD

Man don't she juggle good
      not ordinary like
standin on the spot   but
movin up and down the block
        runnin in the wind
throwin velvet oranges in the air   little green boxes too
    every which way she can
          far as the   eye can see
now she's turnin her back   walkin away
      actin real cool

THERE'S NO WAY NO WAY MAN
SHE CAN CATCH THAT STUFF   NO WAY SHE CAN EVEN SEE
WHERE IT'LL COME DOWN

But oranges is droppin now   droppin everywhere   thick 'n fast
my god   look   she's turnin
runnin back   quick   she's catchin them   oranges
overhand   underhand   loop de loop   bendin in   out
        loose and fast
not stoppin   just turnin   short for a breath
catchin that stuff like crazy   all over   behind bushes
        under rock

The wiz she is   a sight for sore eyes
     headin in now for the last   boxes comin in slow
she needs time with them shapes   her FINALE
      she's doin good   with them boxes
and them boxes   jees   they ain't that easy to catch.

INTERLUDE

Work is done
and now is the time
to learn
how to use the space
left
what to do with the waiting
and
I am back to Sunday child

watching
suspended on   tenterhooks

waiting for cars
company coming

SALMONING

after CS

I have to write
knowing old
is finished
purpose   is
ground for new
being   is salmon
swimming
upstream
to love
their
nether
side

ECHO LAKE, SASKATCHEWAN

Glacier made
inland lake
far way from sea   with
no where to go
(how fitting for me
      to notice)

I plan to write
a memory of hot
Qu'Appelle Valley   sun
shining
lake sparkling
one long afternoon

sun gracious
pulling evening
around himself
water resting. I want to give expression to grace.

            but

I'm not   working out   that way
evening is too tight and
this lake is crowded   with
no where to go
            I remind myself :
      This lake is a metaphor   This is not me
These words are a poem   opening   ground   and

            I am earth
         lake is river
               breaking through me   is resolution
                  at hand.

CHANGING PLACE

Catching hold
back of the Dodge garage on Second Avenue in Saskatoon
(there was hardly room to move)
some thistle took root

Mechanics leaving   if they looked   saw
Dodge   sometimes Chrysler   parts
oil cans   grease   not thistle
smelled   the middle of the earth

            thistle, n. Kind of prickly composite plant
            with a globular or cylindrical   head
            holding purple, yellow or white flowers
            may be compared to ROSE

In Saskatchewan   in the summer
by the side of the road   thistles grow
Almost more than one can bear   they stand
stiff prickly   purple   composite plants   with
unusually beautiful flowers   in globular heads.

PRAIRIE

I am native
poplar
no longer searching
for solid oak
satisfied with small
leaves quivering
breeze
quickening
my heart
is prairie
wind
principle

FALL

                    Sky

                         touches land

          straw coloured
                         straw covered
                    land

LAND SONG

No longer
an observer
part of the land
I belong
my difference unique
the grass and me
equal

Death Is an Anxious Mother

Thistledown Press 1986

STONE DETOUR

Turning
a corner
I am abreast
of a cemetery

stone markers
stand
loosely
relaxed
above ground

make me feel
peace
gathering

in my mind
words

turn over stone

THE SCENE

The church
is old
the colour of ash
later looking taupe
the colour of deep
riverbed
clay

buttresses   fly out
from its roof   low enough
to touch

(it sits
wrong way round
on the block)

a girl about ten
is approaching
she curls
in tall prairie grass
a bird in a nest
her eyes open
and close

rest in a time
she is past

OLD MEMORY IS MIXED

The goat is
sitting on top of an old black car
        crazy king
    of a country   farm   yard   .

    I believe we visit   or
        possibly we live

        in this memory

        my sister calm
        eats potato bugs
        she is three   maybe four
        there is the fuss
        of my mother   ending this

DEEPLY FLAWED

A flaw
is a place

thicker than usual
on   for example
a plate
        where
        translucence
        is gone

        where
        molecules
        gather

        too tight
        together

        they keep out
        light

BE CAREFUL WITH WORDS
after Fred Wah

You cast our   words
       that circle   round
         sound
           hooks
reels me in

       you throw me back   small fish
cast again

        I am stunned   stay
    circling near

        you hook me
once more
     this time
        land me

limp and flat
    I move on

     familiar shore

I'M SUPPOSED TO BE THE POET
after Joe

but it was my son
who said:

I heard
tiny horses
hoof beats
on my window

looked up
and saw
rain

DEATH IS AN ANXIOUS MOTHER

Death is
        an anxious mother
afraid for her kids
        she holds them
        too light   she

can't bear   the chances
        they take

IT FOLLOWS

Don't think
I haven't done this
before: I have   you know
been around   men like you
men who peek out
from sky
blue eyes
(surely magic
since they make me think
they can be touched)
trick me
into believing
before there's time
to know
they're not often out
this way
these men
whose secret
selves are kept
locked inside

their eyes   always
they have sky   blue eyes.

ANOTHER LOVE POEM

Again
   and again
     the same
      rising
       joy

falling
forward

        oh not "head over heels"
        but that's the image
         the real
          image: going out to one another
                 falling
                   forward
           on a gold fall day
                falling
            and rolling
               wrapped together in leaves
         through valleys
        and hills
          rolling and holding each other   no
       not each other
           but the wind
          it is the wind
           we are being held together
         in love
            by the wind

THE MONK

There is something
so good
about holy men

I don't mean those who see
visions

but the ones who know
everything
is on a par

like the one
who said: for constipation
eat popcorn. For God
look everywhere.

SHOPPING
for jl

They are so determined
to make me spiritual
raise me above
my basest habits   but

I am connected to peasant
love to buy
bright purple skirts
wear them   then buy some
more

Marx tells me
I'm conditioned to this
buying
Capitalists   make it so

Freud says
no   it's sublimation
really   I'm avoiding pain

Holy men get their kicks
praying alone   but
bright
stirs my desire

for cloth
tangible
to touch

GETTING UP

Dry prairie grass
late winter
valley hills are soft
bronzed under my feet

I climb and the effort tells: my breathing
comes hard

at the top I can see for miles
all around the lake
paths fork

my direction depends on time   how much I have
to decide

RED EARTH, YELLOW STONE

Thistledown Press 1989

DARK MYSTERY

This is getting out of hand
that is to say
while I   (the person I think of as me)
decide to keep open to you
wonder
who you are   what Jungian
part you're playing
in my life   this body soars
with other ideas   to put it plainly
wants you

and not only that   you

disturb
my correct   world point of view
weigh my mind
with some kind of thick
heavy sense

A FRIEND I CAN TOUCH

I imagine
walking out of the kitchen
with coffee
                feeling good
wanting all that goodness   to move
out to you   standing there

Putting the coffee down
I imagine reaching out
          being
              in your arms and
     I value this
              loving
              a man
       one is permitted
          to touch.

IN A HOUSE WITH YOU

I mean: I say I'm afraid because
                    you're the quiet one

    but
that isn't it   really
                    it's not you
          I'm afraid will cramp my style

          but my own silence   inside
      want to crawl in your body
          sleep there forever

I'm afraid   it'll be me   who
                pulls myself in
                too tight

    creates a you who holds me
                        to death
                pulls my spirit out
                all night

GET IT RIGHT

Marriage, I write
looking it up
in the dictionary, to get it right
I've always had trouble with it, and the word
getting the *i* in the wrong place, mixing it up
with *aige*, making it look like french glue,
or a kind of malaise.

COMMITMENT

How do I get out of it
the party   I mean
what if I invite
everyone
          then decide
I don't want to bother
having all these people
in my house

I mean
it's a modem dilemma

this question of commitment

even five hours
is a trap

the thought of which
shakes me up

PRUNING

I worry this, moving close
feel your every hesitation, actually feel it
like pain, in my bones, the part of you
you hold from me:

  I am becoming
  Japanese, a shrub

              pruned back
        again
        and
        again
    limited   but now
          the image grows
              thick and green

      rich
    in a small
  strange shape

COMING HOME

I am the absence I see, or
    feel in you

it is myself I am missing

the empty place   I want
is my silence

the absence of sound
    ringing

TODLAY IS LOVE

The ancient virgin grass
            is warm   as we lie
                  on this hill   just above
                        the Franciscan monastery

      across the valley
   cattle arrange themselves   so perfect
         they soften my brow   and

      in the sky
            glints of silver
                  swoop

                              disappear

            swoop
            appear
                        again,
      fly so high
         they could be angels
               we catch sight of

   in the dry fall grass
               we lie   looking up
            held in this
            time together

RED EARTH, YELLOW STONE

Adam means earth, red means

        iron is present
      a hard and stable mass

    Yellow means love
another name for grace
        spirit
    that won't stay down

    but stone may crack
    and earth may fall

    vision means risk

    possibility is all

DECIDING

Lying here in these soft hills, bronze grass filling me with
colour, a pale yellow stone calls me to name, beginning.
Comes to me the word: decide. De is a beginning, a prefix
from latin meaning undo. Cide, on the other hand, sets me
back. It is a suffix, an ending. In both latin and french, means
caedere. Killer, slaughterer of ox. Cutter of stone.

Cutter of stone: is a beginning, possibility of mind. Decide is
to undo a cutting, sew up a stone. To undo killing is to give
living. Decide is a word filled with undoing, slaughter, killing
and living.

THE BEGINNING

I picked up a stone that day walking in the hills, it wasn't the first. It was later when I was washing them, all the stones I'd brought home, this one made itself clear to me. Small its shape, and its colour moves away from description, is palest tawny yellow, intermingled not separate from a colour that on its own might be white. Fused cracks or fused flaws contain minute specks of black I imagine in time might wear away.

This description does not account for the appeal of the stone which creates a softness around my neck and down from my ears. Creates a softness in the centre of my encasing soul. My body is my soul the place where spirits enter and rest. My body is my beginning, spirit enfleshed.

TIME COMES TO HOUSES ON SUNDAYS

Going out of my house to work, but wanting to stay
home, wanting a respite, no, something more   smooth
something silent, an interval, an interim, a
                             lunation:
                 long enough
                       for the moon to circle
           a month of Sundays and gold
                            light to shine
                     through blinds
         touching the hard
             wood floor

      A month of Sundays   enough   space
           for a pattern of habit to form
    round the lake   walking
               back to the warm
         fragrance of dinner
                     in the fall
             night comes early

A month of Sundays and time gentles down, urges:
               take it easy, she
       mutes the day, calls attention
       to herself.
           Time reminds
       beyond the world
               she is there
       the fabric
       of day

ANOTHER TIME

My lover, who is a scientist
and only knows the truth, tells me: Time
                        is female, a mother
            holding us
                        all
            in her emanation
            to heaven

AMBER

Amber, found in the Baltic
sea, is pale
fossilized pine
resin washed ashore   or it is
     mixed with a kind of blue
         clay soil

     caught in nets

this translucence   hangs in beads
                    time
held still
     round my neck

HANGED MAN

I write about amber

beads around my neck
              and
remember a boy
who hanged himself when I was ten

                    and another
      memory is loose: Tarot sign   a hanged man
             I grab my pen to change the outcome
             write the words.
             Tarot card: hanging man
                re-
                   lieved I see
                    he's hanging

        all right
          but he's
      hanging
free
  energy
      swinging   and
        smiling
he is swinging and smiling and hanging

             by his foot
           up
             side
         down

ORANGES

Hot, I remember the heat of the day
                stopped in time
                climbing a steep hill
        in one of the old black cars

        then we are parked
                in dust and silence
        in the middle of a prairie town
                in front of a hotel door

I am five years old
                and though they are there
        I don't see my sisters   in this memory
                        only I   am standing
                                by the car
                                door
                                watching

        then he is there
my dad
                and we buy oranges   an offering
                        for my grandmother
                                waiting
                in fast growing dark   and the point
                        the point of this poem:

                I am five, for godsake
        my grandmother meets us, her lamp turned low
        my father hands her oranges, and I know
                        all of this
                offering is wrong

PREY WAS HOLY

There is sitting next to me
on the plane
a man without hands
in their place he has hooks, they
appear to be made
from steel and to grip like claws
or pincers of a memory I have
of a bird or crab
something strong
in my memory
before time created choice
and prey was holy

LANGUAGE, HOPE, MY MOTHER AND ME

The day has passed
just barely got through

      by reaching
     into language
    (a fine dark mystery
   that stays the moment) like a mother

      language
opens her arms   holds me
     craves me from a deep
      deep place
   in a voice that is old
         always she is there
            in time
    disguised
   she is waiting

ANGEL WINGS ALL OVER

Thistledown Press 1994

IMAGINE THE AFTER LIFE
after Ken Lochhead

I am struck (always expected a stroke)
with what I see in the artist's painting, at age 62
there is new life, every variety of it: plant, animal, bird
all come into view from the edge. He paints thick green land
gathers in colour (always two) love angels, birds
and flowers in the sky. All in a garden he paints this

and at the end do we each begin to draw our own afterlife? on
flat gold canvas place the particular   on my canvas

a hen, miniature statue of St. Anne holding Mary as a child.
In my picture this grandmother of God bends to touch the
chicken, steps down from the elevation of her base,
begins to colour, the metal steel turns to rose.
The chicken is small, an English game hen, green and blue.
Baby Mary wants to walk.

The scene expands: covers a whole farm yard; in the back
ground trees grow. Then Anne (she's dropped the St.) checks
on Mary who is toddling to a lake. A mountain goat watches all
from a hill. Fish and frogs jump in the lake where ducks gather.
An eagle flies over, while an otter skirts the earth. A bear
keeps moving at an angle from the back
and over and through the trees the painting goes on.

A SPELL OF IMAGES

When I have these little spells
  that unsettle my balance

I see myself reaching ahead
                      grasping
     for someone and
           around me; only
    the fine thin presence of air

another note
    tells me: I
      thank God
  for these dark and cloudy spells
    where images cluster
            break
  open   inside me
  make me reach
      for something

not easy
          some
            sense
        stopped
       in my mind.

A LONG WAY HOME

Absence grows in me
    blocks of time
   fill me with   space
    all
memory of shape
   gone

a house full of empty
        light
          waiting to be called
        home

MY LEG MEANS TO ME

The leg that hurts,
is on the right side of my body
that side they say is 25% weaker than the other
but the left one too, my witty physiotherapist says,
is not that hot. *Like the old joke*
where the guy who can't have any kids goes to the Dr.
apologetic says: I don't know Doc, maybe I don't have
the right knack. No, says the Doctor, not the left one either.

And today I got a letter from you, someone who knows bodies;
give 100% attention to that leg you said, feel
the truth of it and when you do from that point on
you'll improve. You wrote more but I was impatient and you

ended it
with: It's all in what your leg means to you.

Since then I have been waiting for this time, these moments alone
to ask myself (because I believe you) about my leg.

The first thing that comes into my mind
is the picture on the cover of a book. *Love Stones of One*
Kind or Another, a woman wears a hat of flowers that grow
high above her; the man, the shape of a man, cuts off the legs
of another woman, headless, behind him. The hands
of the man and the woman extend towards one another
but even as they reach standing apart as they do
on the cover of the book they do not touch.

Oh, with a singleness of mind I have reached
even beyond my body to touch you.

Arching over all in the picture is a rainbow.

STONES

The first one gold, found walking in the hills
a holy place, now gone; I put it in a ring.

Then amber crossed the sea in another ring
from Russia via Poland to me.

Stepping stones
to make the walk to my house
easier
        and stone markers
      standing loose, casual
          over graves.

Stones moving up from the earth
everywhere; my grandfather escaping them
moving across the sea,

and gathered from my body after surgery two days ago
290 amber coloured stones, a nurse
placed them in an envelope   called
for my mother to see.

June 12, 1991

THE KITCHEN COLANDER

I clean this old green colander,
brought from another life   one
I always wanted

all the time I mean to clean this colander better
but it's used so often: draining pasta, peas and meat,
anything with juice. Usually I only rinse it
before it's put away.

I am cleaning it now, a day into the New Year, 1989,
after using it to drain asparagus for a casserole
I've made for someone close. It comes clean
almost on its own, sitting in hot water and suds.
I rinse it fresh, wipe it dry, clean the stand really well.

I drained chicken grease in this colander
a long time ago, hot oil; a quarter section of it cracked and
it's been cracked since then

one large hole melted wide extends over three smaller ones
and below in a line of five, three holes there also joined.
A slight colouration extends to the bottom. The lowest part
is fine.

Turning it over I see the colander is rough. I hold it
up to the light coming in the kitchen window   and
rough recedes; I think of a Tarot card, the hanged man,
swinging by his foot, energy flowing through him, bright light.
I stop cleaning   not to overdo it.

AWKWARD ANGEL BLESSINGS

It works this way, the awkward ones, their
great angel wings   sweeping, move grace; like
sand in the air it sticks to your teeth, lodges
on your lips, you find it crusted in hollows
coating your skin   glaze of thin white icing
on a cake, so sweet; they know not what they do
these angels, bumping into one another
trying to be graceful, like the ones who bring messages
trumpet the Lord

awkward angels leave havoc in their wake
fly over wounds   anything that's open   they're
always joking   turning cartwheels
jostling they scatter   one another's hearts

full of grace.

ELVIS SETS IT FREE

for and with Tim and Mary

Elvis, Elvis, Elvis they cried
and I was a teenager when I saw him
above the waist   on TV

this protected us from his power
          to loose sex.

Running now decades later to Elvis playing
ALL SHOOK UP, my tight spine, the small of my back
all shake free : his beat unlocks cells

and there have been sightings too, of this man
like a saint he comes,   apparition in the night.

He looses groins, that's his touch. He sets them free

the other night talking theology,
we spoke of *theandric*, Tim said it's called, the impulse
to call forth in love, in one deep gaze,
a single blade of grass, a man, the truth in each creation.

He looses groins, Elvis does
for God; he repeats it and repeats it
like a saint, he makes that miracle.

EXPLORATION
after HM

She plans to explore in her art work,
the somewhat infrequent but nonetheless constant,
Saskatchewan alkali slough.

These patches can be seen for miles, glistening white, a mirage
always in the offing; driving toward them in a car
they could be ice, snow,   possibly lake. One
would not think   salt.

She wants to explore the meaning of these sloughs
in our land, and me as a child who passed them for years
think of them only as places to miss, their pure white surface
to be avoided at all cost: underneath this salt crust, she agrees,
there is a substance   thick as oil, black that goes
                              away   down deep.

LILAC

for my mother

Walking through the park, stereo cassette playing Vivaldi
in one car, this perfect May morning the lilacs are full
and I pick one ready to drop; its petals so pale; thin

                                        organza
                    I remember   one dress she made
                                light purple flocked with white
each detail clear: the front tucked,   sewn in
parallel folds an inch deep; the collar Peter Pan, skirt gathered
                    with a self belt. A perfect dress
                    A well made garment, she would say,
                                        of a dress someone else
                                                had sewn.

    She
            knew that balance salves souls, softens face,
                        makes a silence inside;

                    she knew   the shape of things
                        is eternal

THE WAY SHE CARED

My mother saying: *God looks after drunks and fools*
when my father left (drinking for days).

and me, the fool not looking,
stepping out into a riding ring
to cross to the other side
horse galloping by
missing me by so little
I feel the moisture of his flesh
strike my neck.

SMALL FEARS
after Adam

Roses in bud, small
yellow birds in a cage   these

tiny breathing graces
signal my brain:

watch out there, don't
do any harm

And in my house, now
drying upside down, three red
roses; in a hurry I am
to salvage them and the memory
of you who gave them to me,
so short, the time ago.

And the cage in the corner
of my kitchen as I write,
in there the birds, your gift
this Christmas

I am afraid to touch.

OLD FRIEND

When I saw him suddenly, absent so long,
I imagined for a moment
we might wed   oh

too many husbands and wives
were behind us   but
                    for that moment   I dreamed
          we were old   the two of us
                              wounds married

GRACE

Grace was diminishing day by day until
any sight of it
would have been named
strange in this house. But this Christmas Day, love
rose from those ashes people speak of when they taste
the grey of blessings gone.

First it was the usual: struggle (that word shapes the way
union in bodies takes place in people like us)
but it happened early this day (we) mixed together.

Then the second: together again
our bodies laughing   skiing over snow round the lake we flew.

Mid afternoon I washed fish for baking,
you made music on the piano
the door opened for children in this small white house

Later   the table crowded with Christmas
family gathered with friends   grace rested

1991

GRACE 2

This morning walking by the lake
on the bank
a round nest of movement   ducks
crowding together in a circle
suddenly there

A GOOD PERSPECTIVE

Grass
grows where it will. Grass
is not rational

Rain loves the earth
comes to her from clouds. Rain
is not rational

Trees have a way of bending to the earth. Trees
are not rational

Wind is not rational

Bones decay into the orderly earth but bones
are not rational

Almost nothing is rational, but

                              rational has a good perspective
loves
         .   to divide, hold everything up
                        to the fresh clean air.   She
is not good though
          for holding children when they are ill   nor
             for   giving self over to sleep

LIGHT CHANGE

Early fall, morning still green
                moist
almost frost last night, season
                    beginning to think
             of change, hesitates
the night too is confused,   with dreams
                          of loss: homeless ones
                    protect a tent with knives
But I move ahead of myself: this morning
             dreams   in my blood   rage a question
        of change, and I am up
            stretching   the aching
                  body moving   into the air
        one step
            in front of the other,
              only that
Leaving the house late, white stucco, my old deck
                  newly stained blue,
    at the back, I stop, sweep
                 drops of water away
     breathe the day, not noticing   until

getting into my small yellow car, looking up
           the loose green of shrubs,
       overgrown, reach to the sky   leaving,
        a space for light   between

ANGELS ALL OVER

The magazines are full of them   easing
    their way between pages,   pushing in
    with their wings as they do;   the last journal
held three, and my own, the old

      Angel of D.
      all a flutter

I shook then waking
        she did   hold me   though
    awkward, both of us
      falling

    angel wings all over

THE MOON

So often I've heard myself
defend the ordinary, talk
about the spirit (of God)
     in
          :bread, cheese and milk, men and
                         women too
        (get the picture)
        no one thing
   better than another, everything
            moving
            but

       when I stop to look up
        tonight   and

                the moon passes   she
                captures me
                only she, the moon
                     alone

Soul To Touch

Hagios 2009

DROUGHT RELIEF

Grass, as we make our way home, late this day
    is ready to break from hiding come
from under the surface, move out from straw covered land
left bare this past winter, no snow these patches are pale

    shadows of hope green on the brink.

Dust devils on my left pictures in a book divide
                right and wrong
          keep their distance so far

    but in the city, wind takes shape, bits of stone
    strike my face, the back of my neck, my legs

    In the morning I linger   after a night trace of rain
    carry in my mind a memory of lake, smell of the sea and

    in the midst of this absence, forced to myself
    I see this desert as home find in my heart room

    my shoulders drop down

    I reach into drought wait for rain
    to weep herself free.

GIFT OF BREATH

I breathe in

breathe

in-

hale

this gift

beyond

my body

gracious as ever

TREES TAKE ACCOUNT OF THE AIR
after St. Peter's Abbey

1.

Walking early morning across the monastery yard
          air   breathing   breeze
              ruffling dark poplar trees already

          I've walked our country road,
          eaten eggs coddled for breakfast,
      found a monk who's found a tape recorder,
          my new song waiting to be sung,

          "Light works as an anointing material,
          works its way, works its way into my body . . . "

2.

              the day barely begun   but alive I hear
      leaves   almost name
          the feeling on my face they are trying
              to say: listen, you are happy. This rustle I take to mean
                          content.

3.

      Trees do not let you down,   oh their leaves bend,   and
          daily   they shake out their grief,   but
  only the rarest tornado can fell one,   pruned well they withstand
              even
                  this;
          trees I think of as answers,   love
              in   solitary monastery   air

THE GRASS AND ME IN THE MORNING
after St. Michael's

Walking again I always start the words
walking
grass tall by the side of the road   tall
by the side of the road that makes its way up the hill   where
Franciscans live
and writers retreat   inside bodies   and   roads
lead everywhere

but back
to the tall green grass   beside me as I walk:

do the blades, each, as I do,
think *to themselves* seeing me beside their prairie nest, on a hill,
does grass think: *does it not*

make sense to think

we, the grass (speaking for itself) and (me) the woman walking
are in love
breathing in and out of one another   this morning
a marriage   with the prairie grass at ease

TWO IN THE SKY, ME IN THE GRASS
St. Michael's

Today   it isn't walking I do my companion her name   grief,
wishes only to lie down, not walk the wild hills my way;
I look for a sign a way to arrest her wound but she closes my eyes, says,
I need all your attention, lie down on this grass, imagine you're home
take care of me still. And I do, lie on the grass on the side of a hill,
forget about time   I may even sleep.

A narrative line wants to come into this poem   can you imagine space
in the middle of time

when I open my eyes up to the sky I think
it must be a hawk flying so high swooping in circles
behind clouds and I follow, and follow   then there are two
hawks in the air swooping and arcing   and lifting
a skim from my heart leaving a wound open to air and
tomorrow two of a kind watch as I pass
deer on the path   we cross.

DRIVING HOME YESTERDAY

Stunned by the prairie
yesterday

green and shining grasses   bending

arched beneath sky, blue scented so fresh, and
this barely begins
to draw the surround that loosed my heart, stilled

my mind driving home   another
funeral; my old aunts dying
one by one   I couldn't write this

but today, a seminar, I picked up this pen — for distraction — and

prairie fell into place   my mother   alive
in my memory of summer
wheat fading to gold   bruised ripe
the scent of fall   autumn smoke
the wonder of it
an actual place,
a real location my body calls home.

THE NATURE OF LOSS

Lying in bed this morning
empty of hope
imagination   gone silent
missing a picture: the way horses lean into one another

necks rubbing   as the wind
carries on around them,
or the way
a tiny bee loses himself deep in the heart of a golden flower

GIVING UP THE HOUSE

What it comes down to isn't the up-keep
　　　though that's a point,
　　　　　no
　　　　　　　it's the illusion
this house contains: beyond reason it holds
more years to come or at least it did
until last night when the furies arrived, sat before me
looked me straight in the eye, wasted my soul,
roused my own rage at age
Gods take away everything: smooth face of skin, energy of bone,
　　delight of eye, oh yes houses they leave

AS I HURRY DOWNTOWN TODAY

Through the park
walking fast   downtown
first spring day   I pass a woman
walking carefully clearly
her degenerative body
dis-ease
slows her but see   she is
at ease
and I imagine her:
carrying her books back to a library, as she does,
breathing this warm morning air, feeling
compassion for me
rushing past   as I do.

THE MOON DRAWS
after Rae Johnson

The moon draws   oh yes
she can draw all right
I've seen her at night slipping to earth
gathering roots and stone   to make her paints

she piles on colour thick green and blue she paints thin
trunks of trees   men too
she draws forward to her own (white) reflection in water and
black
earth shadows she slicks back from trees while her men hold on for
dear life
urged to the water   drawn there by the moon
but see though she has created this earth rolling
she has those shadows hold everything still.

THE DRAWING

The drawing where I live is pale,
a kind of ripe autumn gold, a shade of wheat
bronze in colour.

You can see me there
if you look carefully, see

just at the edge a small shape,
once shaded dark outlined now
but still needing to be filled in.

RED FOX

I've read through the whole book, it wasn't difficult
    really: catlike canine, the idea of a red that glows,

burnished brick,

      sometimes crossed with black, sandy when young,
           having charcoal natal fur,
        a natural predator over ages lasting

    the first one *(Red)*

moved me to further search,
and I found the other, *Swift,* had grown separate over the years
its family becoming slightly different.

SWIFT FOX, NEARLY EXTINCT
for DG Jones

There are other animals
more appealing, more easily sweet, you might say,
valiant but oh
Swift Fox you capture me

not so much   I agree with you
in fact your fox eyes I do not prefer

It's the idea: you even have paws, cross-over
Canine body close to cat

In certain light, ears spread beyond your tiny body, bat, in silhouette
illusive Basenji Egyptian dog.

Most people, my lover says, use nature as metaphor for mood
but you are metaphor for wild and

what does any of this mean; an idea of God, mystery
in which we live everything mixed nothing so clearly separate
as we might think.

FALLING INTO THE SKY
after Emily Dickinson

Saying yes   to a poem
about Emily, writing her back or   simply
responding   the invitation said   simply respond   and Emily is
                    slipping   out of her house   to her porch
            at dusk   coupling   with the tender night air   in love
she glows

        can't keep it straight   doesn't even try   she mixes her words
            with birds   and God   the air we all breathe   and

my grandson, Thomas, says: the world is turning
                everything moving   so fast
                a person could fall into the sky   Emily   too

        is falling
in love   with the sting of a star screaming past   afraid
she writes   every particle of the world touching her skin and the sky

            this cold winter: Emily's words   soft as stones (set down
                on a summer cloth)   slip into my heart
                                undivided
                she writes the birds of the sky the stars
                she writes   the very air together.

BACON LOVER PRAYER
after Catherine Bush

You are gone   oh yes
we may unite again but there is emptiness
coming into this house

in the evening:
your absence is strong   but

this morning, Sunday, when we might have been making love
I am eating reheated bacon on thin crisp toast   reading
a review of a book that contains
my migraine malady that strange land of colour

but it's the bacon I feel   how truly good
this sandwich   taste rising as it does in this moment
moving through me and above everything this pleasure
deserving its own small praise

EVERGREEN MIRRORS MY SONG

Turning the corner
    en route over mountain roads
        music in my car
            Buffy Sainte-Marie singing from her throat
            and before me
                mirroring her vibration,
                    herringbone row upon row

                                        evergreen

trees repeat and
    beside me
        the head of a single yellow rose
        I carry this totem from one
            not easily given to the practice of love

            but today slipping through sun
            my heart is in his hands driving

I. BECOMING: A HEART

Walking in the early steep
part of the path on Sleeping Buffalo
some still call it Tunnel Mountain
it comes to me to write
when I get back to my room: no matter
which way you cut it I am
a woman, without doubt
I have breasts and though small
they did give forth at least once

I plan
still breathing (too) hard to write
more of me, a man in me
as I walk, the one
whose picture I scribble over
each time he begins to hint a shape

then here at a corner
near the top, stopped in a bit of shade
for breath on the tree I lean against
directly at eye level
not carved but worn away in a shade of rust, a heart
its colour deeper than its pale rose shape surround.

What to make of it: male and female and a heart, *rose*, and the note
back in my studio quoting a writer asking me to read
the signs, and the other one: *writing, is writing, is writing,*
all this on my path, sun unusually hot
without clouds this year for tempering
cedar berries lush for the picking when suddenly
ill with it all
I turn slowly back and down
hoping for time to return

4. FALLING OVER MYSELF

Grass in nature, lasting long
but growing only so high
      carried by the weight of itself
         falling
           down

   down
      and gently over
              blades

resting on one another   a family at ease.

8. THE DECK GOD

I sit on my deck   today
circling in on God
from behind my studio watch grass reach up; shoots
rest each on one another   leaning forward they bend
in places where elk nest lay their great bodies down

       today
beginning is
full of cloud   but warmed beyond hope touched
by this gift   my soul is making (concrete) words whole

12. THE VIOLA PLAYER

Later I would see she was unusually tall, her nature
a weather warning   bleak

For a change I faced this; stared her ill manners down
spoke about my affection for the viola,
an instrument she played. Why, she asked, and when I said I resonated
to the sound, she asked again, why. And I turned
the question, asked the same of her. It sounds awful, she said, played badly
but played well it's necessary to the orchestra.   No one
picks it out as something special but if it's missing   you know it's gone.

It links all the other instruments, like its partner the bassoon
it's not spectacular but it is necessary   for connection.

VICTORIA, birthday

I used to write a poem on my birthday   an annual
   welcome to myself so to speak and today

here by the sea near a duck pond and a bridge
                a long way from my north and
                prairie home
      I do write

More peaceful
        than ever   and
              I have known   peace:

      once long ago   when night terror
         seized me in sleep too deep to survive

      I felt myself slipping away   and
            as I was falling felt
   someone entering, filling my room, me, filling everything
   with such peace *its texture was velvet*   but

         what does any of this mean this
   grace that story   here by the sea   those I love at home

MY HEART HOLDS STILL

The right thing to do if you love   and I do
is let go   the right thing to do if you love

send him on his way, wish him well, set him free

I have done all of this, even said the words   out loud.
It's my heart won't let go   beyond any sense
my heart holds him   still.

EVERYTHING IS IMMANENT
after A.

1.

At the Butchart Gardens this spring
   millions of buds are pulsing
     crowded inside
petals of colour   near bursting and
on this well tended path   my body feels
     such longing,
you with me here and this garden would be
     animated

2.

Today, another garden, the Abkhazi
  more gentle than yesterday red
lichen furled tight against rock succulent lips
     pursed to the sky
  your absence shadowing me

      escaping

3.

  like my mother finding comfort in a cathedral
   I find my way to a picture gallery:
     and these paintings
    still my soul
    bring me back   and all things missing

4.

      pale
    in the face of these man made creations
      and lichen
  the way cells find a pattern hold memory
  tight to rock   plump themselves up to light

WAKING UP ALONE

At first *dawning; no, the dawn comes later*
         at first   waking
             everything as usual   as though beside me
    lies a man
   I would spend the day with   spend   the   day
its coins: another body   walking with me in the sun
    by the sea   and all the other *trivialities*   he called
my coffee, walk by the water, music: Martha Wainwright, and her
brother,
Rufus
    singing,
         but as I stretch   truly waken
         today my streets waken too   and
         in bits of my body
         tiniest cells are becoming

TIME AND BEING

Here alone:
there being nothing else to be   I am
here   alone   reading   and reading   *negation*

Heidigger, being German, has   on *his* own
hit upon
what Buddhists — not to mention farmers in their fields —
call *detachment,* that fortunate space *one may be given,*   not
knowing
answers,   or even questions,

that moment   (alone)

when warm air strikes your face, that's *the warm air
created by the earth*   going round and round
nowhere but

nonetheless turning   in earnest   turning and asking
*has someone removed the rail
I was meant to ride upon?*

the earth turning and turning, until
one thing after another,
all things wear out,
once in awhile *seeing an opportunity* the earth
shifts

just for a moment
and stepping back
every
thing
falls
cells lie quiet

all we know is at rest
and in this

empty

(Heidegger calls negation)   all springs forth

THE PACES OF LOVE
after r.

    You don't know at first when you meet them,
angels on the job; one landed here I'm pretty sure he was old
Archangel
    Gabriel:

        he didn't mention his name *uses another one for earth*
            not to draw attention though he's very tall.

You can tell
    they've been here by the *upsidedownway* you feel. He

    shook the best of me together
    took me through the twists and turns
    pace of love but you can't marry an angel
    (Arch or otherwise) *wings get in the way* and besides
    all things end though strangely I found in him myself
    strangely able to *let go* love from afar

    come to think of it   *being an angel*
he's not likely to be lost

NOT A QUESTION OF LOVE
after A.

We loved our dad   us kids
nothing
could stop us   but when he wanted a companion
for his wild prairie rides
we declined.

Not that you are my dad or even
for that matter a drinker:
you have other issues   *don't we all* so   though I can't stop
loving you

neither can I
join you for one of those rides   a life time   long

A COMMISSIONING OF WORDS
after the Art Gallery of Regina

    Make
small marks on paper put down code unlock colour   with words

              waiting
         to shape   the space we need to see:

my mother under duress
    my mother under the word duress praying the rosary each evening
      with her sister she fingers her beads roped together they touch
            the sides of her hands, keeping calm.   And

        each person in the world,   *I see*
      laying hands   each upon a particular bead   and
       into each bead unraveling the weight of their fear   grey
         held tight against a pale shade of hope and
lying in bed undone these nights
I think of my mother and her sister   lying silent
        reach for a pen   make marks on this page   shape words
      one after another
            but tonight not words   only

      intention   gesture of arm   staying the course
you can see there for yourself on the wall beyond black is light.

THE FABRIC OF DAY

New Poems

DREAMING THE ACTOR, WALTER MATTHAU

I'm considering getting to know Walter Matthau
in my dream last night,
it was possible;   he is large
unkempt   you could say,   though he's trying:
has trimmed his beard, even straightened his nose
and this all happened   before   I lay with him,   startled
by the peace of it, he makes me happy, and so I ask him,
what might I do for you. He says, *your happiness is my pleasure,*
and then the dream stops, not like a poem which I'd like to be
more open-ended.

TREES LEAN

We were supposed to be

only friends, that was the plan

but I found myself
                    leaning into you

like a tree

whose leaves reach out
                              falling

into the sweet
           sustaining air

LET LOVE LOOSE

You need to watch   when love gets   loose,
      you could   find yourself
         gardening   like mad
           tripping off
                   to Canadian Tire
        to buy a rough mop   to clean your deck
    and that's only the beginning
      it's everywhere,   love

     in the backyard   the front too
          even beyond   and
 no one   ever told you   it was so simple,
        letting go

ANXIETY

If it didn't conjure fear, Anxiety
could be a name, soft   like   Charity,
or Felicity, what I mean to say (got sidetracked).
Anxiety,
when there is nothing to fear,
is a garden, with crows   overhead
flying at your eyes, pecking your arms,
squalling, while you keep on planting
or try to, hoping
they'll fly away, or if not
       simply land

PERSONA CHOICES

Here we are, in the background,
waiting for her to decide
where she's going, what she'll do;
which one of us she'll choose:
her nakedness needs our cover, else
all will see   the fear
our costumes keep   her at bay.

RETIRING, GONE MISSING

One (that one would be me) one would think
one could get one's head read,
see a shrink, say a prayer, even have an X-Ray
there are many ways

to find the part *of oneself* felt
    missing

it's a puzzle at this late stage, a nuisance,
really, feeling the self, one used to be
      gone.   oh
nice to think of this
                absence as a clearing,
all the roles retired (no distractions)
nevertheless it's odd
being with the stranger   I am
                      becoming.

ENNUI

No pattern exists, it comes
late morning, mid-afternoon, evening
a fatigue   that calls you
to lie down   anywhere
sleep   and
            sleep welcomes you
 in a way you might even   call
              delicious
        giving you over, as it does,
       to particulars   vanished

YOU ARE GONE

Waking   what the heck is going on   the air
                    quiet
              calm all around
        Nothing to do   but   get out of bed   strange silence
        all through the house
                    too tired to *serve the Lord*
              or anyone
I can think of:
              companies used to place mechanical *governors*
              inside car motors to keep their employees
                          from driving fast.
                    this morning
        absence of pain;   my governor   gone.

TIME AWAY

after Jacqueline

Time away, she said, I need time away
from the ordinary; she hopes to meet
the girl she once was, the woman she was to become

So she walks the tall grass,
at night listens to her music; thinks
if she keeps her focus,   silent like a cat
that girl   might be sighted.

MEMORIAL

after K

Someone read Simone Weill   on obligation: we are called
to be present;   someone else read Nelson Mandala
            on the gift of being one's self,   not
shadowing another   but allowing   the necessity
                  within each body to become.
There were poems: ships   sail   out of sight   only to be seen
      arriving   we know not where,   but destination
            gives greeting   and
      the night before canoes sailing through the air,
      in the art gallery,   above and around us   and me
dreaming   that night: being seen by another galaxy
as a fish swimming   clothed in ether.   But what do we know,
      what do the particles of our brains really know;
      reading Wade Davis, all the languages gone missing from earth,
      that mystery, that particular story   dismembered.

TAKING A BREAK

Exhausted
        with cleaning, lying on my couch
I open my eyes, to
           fecund,
through my window,
        the word seeps in
              green,
        heavy branches
waving   in this
      late   fall breeze.

THE BODY IS GOD'S POSITION

    Night time
   and my body   waits
  for day and small garden worms
reach up from earth   to hot
     hot sun,   and trees overhang my garden

   watching from my kitchen window
inside and out   my flesh alive to this least
    God's position

This morning cool,
looking out my kitchen window

  in this prairie place
  birds, specific to my back garden,
ferret   for the tiniest seeds
    dip
          and   dip,
between   blades of grass, under gold-coloured leaves
    find   whatever's fallen

WE TRIED TO GROW
after A.

Green leaves, lush, the edges dark;
I think of you, as I re-pot this plant
now thick with leaves

once, it was cramped, tight in soil;
leaves dropping as fast as they grew.

I think of you now   away by the sea,
me here   alone,   as our plant thrives

REAL WINTER
for Jill

Now
real winter is here,
          clear   crisp   ice
cold
      held   in place   by sun, not blazing,   but shining   steady
             so bright   snow   glistens   and
             my daughter says:
  I see   a poem coming on, something
I hadn't   thought
    to make   this   first day
             of real winter,   snow
          covering   ground   where thick wet sludge
             had   blocked the city   for days

HOW I ALMOST MARRIED LEONARD COHEN

"You almost married Leonard Cohen," they said,
long after the 70s when their dad and I separated;

    They'd remembered Leonard, always in the house,
      seeing me   alive in his songs, thought
    we'd make a good pair,   so one night
        they gathered
           to write the letter:

"She loves your music," they said, "and we think
    with your songs, and the way she thinks
        you'd be a good match."

I asked how it was I didn't know this:

They said they couldn't remember why they hadn't sent the letter;
They'd all liked the idea, but the thought, the thought, had simply faded.

BLUE PICTURES
after Wilf

Pictures of blue   side by side
snow piled high,   and in another room
blue   turns to summer night,
     a tractor   put away,
      and me,
    a kid from the city, caught   in this
apricot blue   darkening sky
      ending   the day

EITHER OR

When your stomach won't hold
and your legs are weak   your very nature in question
the only thing you think to make the shaking stop
a man   (the way
an addict would say: only this may give me peace)
This longing   of course   is not love
which has a different way about it; love
        likes to be   caught
        unaware,   so to speak

A NAME TO CALL HOLY

When you waken, sometimes
in a strange place,   want   sometimes
to give yourself over
to the fear

find peace in the trembling
sometimes want to   call out
a name
beyond yourself
in the face of this

THE WEDDING IS OVER
after J and B

The wedding is over,
celebrations   before and after   all gone but
memory   wants the guests to stay, wants
                the parties back, nothing for it
memory is a hard bargain;   can't tell her a thing, but today

without notice,   suddenly   she stops
body limp, no way to say it;   just stopped, left me alone
and   I woke up   no engine   outside
to set me straight   caboose shunted   off track
exactly where I am

THE STRENGTH

Lying in Bed, this morning
      trying to catch   hold
      find a way   to make sense
find courage
    to live the long haul; a man
        (I love) dying.
Lying in bed
        thinking
the world is
   as it is, nothing can change
     the consequence of birth, but now
     in my body   I have to travel
       to this man, and
 where is strength for that? Then the words
     floating up   *from where?*

   "Be not be afraid," "I will give you rest,"
and through my body   a whole
    communion of saints   embedded
          come into my life, and
   I travel, even as the dying goes on.

JIGSAWS
after Jeannie

In my mother's seniors' complex, large ladies
glance up from jigsaw puzzles; and
my sister and I entering the elevator
giggle, "Shoot me if you see me doing that."
But here I am today waiting for my body
to heal, surgery minor, but home for days   nothing
left to do, I begin a puzzle: blue sky
got me started, startling blue above gold, and more gold
below, so many shades,   and now with all the edges
together I can move within   the Cathedral frame.

CAME UPON IT SUDDENLY

All the signs were there, and   there:
the eyes were first (migraine, bad for years
doesn't count) then   the last time
 my knee flared, I remember, it took more time
 to heal; and there was that questionable kidney;
nonetheless, it did come as a surprise,
 the day I fell into it, my age,

MIGRAINE, LOVE THAT LIGHT

Manifest is a word
that needs
the time it takes to unfold
from
what's been growing
inside
until, like   a plump seed, it bursts and
the right side of your head
is blazing

THE CROSS

One of those mornings, always a surprise,
if not a shock, the old fears have found their way
during the night   and this morning
a body limp, but tingling with   pain

You talk yourself out of it, say,
it's nothing   everything will be
fine   and this works, more or less; you
are up, showered, ready for coffee but before
you set out for your café you rifle through a drawer,
straighten things   looking for . . . what?   Then
alone at home you laugh out loud: you've found the cross
taken from your mother's room, the day she died
the one, rested on her coffin

And there he is
 in bronze: loin cloth, crown of thorns and all;
one tiny arm, nailed as tightly to the cross
as the other, but that arm is wrapped, and wrapped,
my mother has wrapped this tiny arm, thick with tape,
now yellow with time, and the little arm, the poor
little arm   is barely chipped.

What to do with it
this parcel
stowed
one way or another,
over the years   stuck
in this closet   or that
Sorting now, to give the house
a clean sweep, so to speak,   wondering
again,   (standing in the centre hall)
which direction to take,
where to put this
parcel down
wondering   really,
where does regret belong

PHILOSOPHY AT THE DINNER TABLE
for Thomas

We're eating dinner   talking about due-dates,
  bar codes *Best Before* on food packages: When did we start
                    to pay attention ?

                    I say,   before dates
we had to sniff food   for freshness,   but
        before   I can go on
  Thomas   is asking,   what was it like Nana,
                    before dates?
          could you tell   winter from summer,
                    day from night
                the difference between.

THE SHELF PAPER POEM

Down on my hands and knees, well, one knee,
the other, aching, I hold inches above the floor;
this requires some effort, but I am nearly finished
tacking paper on round Lazy Susan shelves   and

I find myself thinking,
as I master this gymnastic feat,

three years after moving into this townhouse,
which took me three years to find, the townhouse
I mean, with a garden.

I find myself thinking, the reason for this tacking
shelves will stay clean, but it's the other,
my desire, (*desire?*) for someone,

to be happy
with what I've left behind   *though*

I do find the idea odd,

here in my kitchen: me, pleased
with leaving a clean Lazy Susan
for some future stranger, stranger
not even thinking   of a poem.

ALREADY WRITTEN
for Nijole

Here   at Oak Bay Marina
wild grasses   turning yellow
lean over themselves,

reveal   a rogue rose bush,
flowerless;   purple stem   standing stiff
inking   a line in the dusky   sky

WRITING POETRY IN LIGHT
after Gail Chin

        . . . the other picture is more green
    but I choose to keep   the first,
       same brilliance   but shaded
    with mist, like a thought   before speech
            and
as I turn away   there   another picture   waves
    unbroken on water   pussy willows
  so still a picture resting,   within itself
      and yet
  and yet   . . .   if a wound is an opening,   there
in the picture   on the water,   barely visible,
      bits of black and white
  pushing me
lower, to the front of the picture,   and again
   pussy willows
       standing perfectly still,   a poem
         in early spring
or is it the water   unbroken   that moves me

JEANNIE SWIMMING

The day is not so hot
as expected,   still
Jeannie comes to swim   and
the clouds move,   you might say,
                                dissolve
            into clear blue   sky, becomes
the air we breathe, no longer
visible, like those of us whose years   ache us back
into each moment   born

NORTH MEMORY
for Noni

Opening the curtain, two deer
curled together, look up from space
shoo them away, my landlord said; but I simply stand and stare
then,   ballerinas, they lower their heads, silently rise

slip away, and I remember that day
with my sister picking raspberries, in the woods,
deer coming close to our grandmother's garden.
everywhere, the scent of pine lingering

THE MIDDLE OF NOWHERE

The sky in the middle of nowhere is huge, and
blue, the bluest *blue*   ever

the land is green, goes on forever, or at least
as far as the eye can see, in fall everything gives way
to gold, before turning   white

in the middle of nowhere   winter is hard, *oh*   sky remains blue
that's a blessing, and the sun shines

brighter than you can imagine, but   white
                                             cold
              seizes your heart (strikes you numb)   and
         there's no place to go   in the middle of nowhere
                            everywhere

THE REMBRANDT LECTURE
after Tim Long

It's Rembrandt we're meant to know,
(the path he took), the way he painted
stately burghers in his town, until irritated
the whole lot of them, his hubris or theirs;
it matters not,   in the end he was left alone
to paint   only himself over   and over
again   until he brought flesh and bone
    his existence, *Rembrandt*, real.

SPACE BETWEEN
reading *Proust was a Neuroscientist*

They say   all the action comes   not
from DNA,   stuff supposed to tell   who we are, but
from space between. Some even say God is proven in this
will   to change
                    direction   unpredicted.

They say   the food chain may exist   without us,
                    but not without a crawling spider.
Some say   artists lay down   what they see
                    outside   but others say
they work to lay down what is not visible, but
                    what is   trying   to escape   from within

THE DARK SIDE, REDUX
after CW

Not a dark side after all, more like
      one of the many

      spaces

   inhabiting our bodies . . . or

      one of the spaces
     our bodies inhabit;
like the location for love,
happiness
      or compassion.

We knew dark was there, "conceptually,"
saw it in others, sure it meant no good.

     But now   I feel dark leading me (she leads me)

    lonely (all those years) that part of me,
     wanting to be known, oh,
        willing to be used;

  for sure   you could say
even "constituted" for wrong

But she whispers
    this space is only human
        possibility;

    soil that can be used
for nothing more than to know   it's there
    creating you whole.

BODY GOING HOME

I could be blindfolded,   driving,
        making my way, as I do
                this city,   my
            second skin
        ice
                    breaking on the lake   (the other lake
was bound by hills)   but this one   meanders   into my city, and
        out again, bound only   by all the land
                bound by sea